NOVENA
JOURNALS

54 DAY
ROSARY NOVENA

prayer journal

NOVENA

intention

START DATE / /

END DATE / /

ANSWERED / /

27 DAYS OF *petition*

1

petition

Ⓙ|Ⓙ*

DATE / /

DAY 1 / 54 ✓

* | Please see the appendix for the 54 Day Rosary Novena Tracking Guide

2

petition

Ⓢ|Ⓢ

DATE / /

DAY 2 / 54 ◯

3

petition

DATE / /

DAY 3 / 54

4

petition

(J)|(L)

DATE / /

DAY 4 / 54

5

petition

DATE / /

DAY 5 / 54

6

petition

G | S

DATE / /

DAY 6 / 54

7

petition

(J)|(G)

DATE / /

DAY 7 / 54 ◯

8

petition

Ⓢ|Ⓛ

DATE / /

DAY 8/ 54 ◯

9

petition

Ⓖ|Ⓙ

DATE / /

DAY 9 / 54 ◯

10

petition

DATE / /

DAY **10** / 54

11

petition

(S)|(G)

DATE / /

DAY 11 / 54

12

petition

G | L

DATE / /

DAY 12 / 54

13

petition

J | J

DATE / /

DAY 13 / 54

14

petition

Ⓢ|Ⓢ

DATE / /

DAY 14 / 54 ◯

15

petition

DATE / /

DAY 15 / 54

16

petition

J | L

DATE / /

DAY 16 / 54

17

petition

DATE / /

DAY 17 / 54

18

petition

DATE / /

DAY 18 / 54

19

petition 

DATE / /

DAY 19 / 54

20

petition

DATE / /

DAY 20 / 54

21

petition

Ⓖ | Ⓙ

DATE / /

DAY 21 / 54 ◯

22

petition

Ⓙ | Ⓢ

DATE / /

DAY 22 / 54 ○

23

petition

DATE / /

DAY 23 / 54

24

petition

Ⓖ|Ⓛ

DATE / /

DAY 24 / 54 ◯

25

petition

DATE / / **DAY 25** / 54 ○

26

petition

Ⓢ|Ⓢ

DATE / /   **DAY 26** / 54 ◯

27

petition

DATE / /

DAY 27 / 54

27 DAYS OF
thanksgiving

28

thanksgiving

J | L

DATE / /

DAY 28 / 54 

29

thanksgiving

DATE / / DAY **29** / 54

30

thanksgiving

DATE / /

DAY 30 / 54

31

thanksgiving

DATE / /   **DAY 31** / 54

32

thanksgiving (S)|(L)

DATE / / **DAY 32** / 54 ○

33

thanksgiving

Ⓖ | Ⓙ

DATE / /   **DAY 33** / 54 ◯

34

thanksgiving

Ⓙ | Ⓢ

DATE / / DAY **34** / 54 ◯

35

thanksgiving

DATE / /　　DAY 35 / 54

36

thanksgiving

DATE / /

DAY 36 / 54

37

thanksgiving

DATE / /

DAY 37 / 54

38

thanksgiving

DATE / /

DAY 38 / 54

39

thanksgiving

DATE / /

DAY 39 / 54

40

thanksgiving

(J) | (L)

DATE / /

DAY 40 / 54 ◯

41

thanksgiving

Ⓢ | Ⓙ

DATE / /

DAY 41 / 54 

42

thanksgiving

G | S

DATE / /

DAY 42 / 54

43

thanksgiving

DATE / /

DAY 43 / 54

44

thanksgiving

Ⓢ | Ⓛ

DATE / /

DAY 44 / 54 ◯

45

thanksgiving

DATE / /

DAY 45 / 54

46

thanksgiving

DATE / /

DAY 46 / 54

47

thanksgiving

Ⓢ | Ⓖ

DATE / /

DAY 47 / 54 ◯

48

thanksgiving

DATE / /

DAY 48 / 54

49

thanksgiving

J | J

DATE / /

DAY 49 / 54

50

thanksgiving

DATE / /　　**DAY 50** / 54

51

thanksgiving

G | G

DATE / /

DAY 51 / 54 ◯

52

thanksgiving

DATE / /

DAY 52 / 54

53

thanksgiving

S | J

DATE / /

DAY 53 / 54

54

thanksgiving

DATE / /   **DAY 54** / 54

the end

OF THE NOVENA

appendix

54 DAY ROSARY NOVENA TRACKING GUIDE

This Rosary Mystery tracker is for the **original 54 Day Rosary Novena** that includes the following Mysteries:
Joyful - **J**
Sorrowful - **S**
Glorious - **G**

This Rosary Mystery tracker includes **the Luminous Mysteries**
J - Joyful
S - Sorrowful
G - Glorious
L - Luminous

The stage of the novena to indicate which novena prayers to pray (i.e. petition or thanksgiving) for that day

A checkbox to tick after finishing the novena prayers for that day

23 DAYS TO THANKSGIVING PRAYERS

A countdown to the 'thanksgiving' stage of the novena

Made in the USA
Monee, IL
01 November 2022

16940989R00070